Biology Pamphlets
by Unknown

Copyright © 2019 by HardPress

Address:
HardPress
8345 NW 66TH ST #2561
MIAMI FL 33166-2626
USA
Email: info@hardpress.net

CONTRIBUTIONS FROM THE HULL BOTANICAL LABORATORY. IX

A CONTRIBUTION TO THE LIFE HISTORY OF THE PONTEDERIACEÆ

WILSON R. SMITH

CHICAGO
The University of Chicago Press
1898

BIOLOGY LIBRARY

A CONTRIBUTION TO THE LIFE HISTORY OF THE PONTEDERIACEÆ.[1]

WILSON R. SMITH.

(WITH PLATES XIX–XX)

THE following investigation of *Pontederia cordata* was begun in the winter of 1897 as supplemental to a course in the special morphology of monocotyledons, under the direction of Dr. John M. Coulter. In the following summer, for purposes of comparison, I collected and studied material of *Eichhornia crassipes*. This is, so far as I know, the first examination of the gametophyte generation of any of the Pontederiaceæ. While the results, as might be expected, do not show any wide deviation from the usual series of events in monocotyledons, they have a value as indicating the extent of variation within a given order, and, in the case of Eichhornia, within a given species.

I wish here to acknowledge my indebtedness to Dr. Coulter for criticisms and valuable suggestions:

EICHHORNIA CRASSIPES.

MICROSPORES.

Fig. 30 represents a cross section of one of the youngest anthers I obtained. The tapetum is a distinct layer of small cells closely adherent to the spore mother cells, and often wedged in among them. Outside the tapetum are usually five layers of wall cells, the innermost of which appears always to disintegrate before the tapetum gives any clear signs of collapse. It is well known that in their later stages the tapetal cells of anthers are likely to become binucleate. Such a condition I have never found in a single case either in Eichhornia or in Pontederia. In the ripe anther there are, as usual, two layers in the wall, the

[1] Contributions from the Hull Botanical Laboratory. IX.

inner of which has the characteristic reticulate thickenings of an endothecium.

The mother cells are very large in comparison with the surrounding cells. About the time they break apart and become rounded, there is a very considerable increase in size. The chromatin assumes a beaded structure and the nucleus enters into the synapsis stage, which has been frequently described in mother cells. The chromosomes, when first distinguishable, are thick and irregular, and lie scattered about in the nuclear space. When arranged in the equatorial plate they have become more regular in outline and can be counted readily. The number is sixteen (*fig. 32*), and the same number appears in the second division (*fig. 35*). This is the reduction number. Although I have not been able to count with certainty the chromosomes in the ordinary vegetative nuclei, I have ascertained the number to be not far from thirty.

Successive stages in the two divisions which end in the formation of the microspores are shown in *figs. 31–36a*. The divisions, as common in monocotyledons, are successive, each daughter cell forming a wall about itself before the second division. So far as observed, the nuclei resulting from the first division do not enter into a resting condition. Very frequently they have no nucleoli, and in such cases there are numerous bodies in the cytoplasm which stain like nucleoli (*fig. 34*). These bodies may also be seen in the cytoplasm even when a distinct nucleolus is present within the nuclear membrane.

The usual arrangement of the tetrads is shown in *fig. 36* (*cf. 35* and *35a*), but such a grouping as *36a* is quite common.

As the microspores continue to enlarge they assume an ellipsoidal shape. The generative and tube nuclei, very unequal in size, first appear when the flowers are about one-third grown; but their origin from the primitive microspore nucleus I did not succeed in observing. The cytoplasm about the small generative nucleus is organized into a clearly outlined spindle-shaped cell, which becomes longer and longer as the microspore matures, until its ends thin out into whip-like filaments (*fig. 40*). Its cytoplasm at the same time becomes highly granular (*figs. 40, 41*).

Another peculiarity of the microspores is the frequent occurrence of a division of the tube nucleus (*figs. 41, 41a*). It is impossible to regard either of the large nuclei of *fig. 41* as a sister of the generative nucleus. The latter is set apart within a separate cell quite early in the history of the microspore, and keeps a constant outline and appearance whether or not the third nucleus is present. Furthermore, the two free nuclei are too large to be so explained, and are alike in every particular, having all the characters by which the tube nucleus is usually distinguishable. Each has a prominent nucleolus, and shows an erythrophilous reaction in staining with haematoxylin and erythrosin, while the generative nucleus has no nucleolus, very abundant chromatin, and cyanophilous staining.

So far as I know, a division of the tube nucleus has been recorded only by Dr. Chamberlain[2] of this laboratory in the case of *Lilium Philadelphicum*, where its occurrence is rare. In Eichhornia, however, fully half of the mature pollen grains examined exhibit this peculiarity. The fate of these tube nuclei, and whether or not there is a division of the generative cell in the pollen tube, I did not succeed in determining. In longitudinal sections through the style pollen tubes were easily seen traversing three central canals, but almost always they showed marks of disintegration. Since Eichhornia does not set seed in our latitude, and there are apparently no abnormal structures in the embryo sac, it is probable that the division of the tube nucleus is due to pathological conditions in the pollen grains, and the failure to produce seed should be ascribed to the same cause.

MEGASPORES.

The youngest flowers obtained had the carpels already fused in such a way as to contain three loculi, and in each of these two longitudinal ridges run along the central axis. These ridges are the six placentæ. The only sign of the ovules at this time

[2] Life history of Lilium Philadelphicum. BOT. GAZ. 23 : 423–430. 1897.

perceptible is the undulated outline of the placenta as seen in longitudinal section (*fig. 1*). In older flowers the placentæ have become distinctly papillate. The dome-shaped prominences shown in *fig. 4* are the young ovules. They are not arranged in regular rows, but are scattered so that every cross section runs through two, three, or four to each placenta.

At this time, or a little later, the archesporial cell is first apparent. Its nucleus is larger and less deeply stained than those of the surrounding tissue, while its cytoplasm is more dense and stains more deeply, especially with erythrosin (*fig. 5*). As the ovule enlarges the archesporial cell divides unequally by a periclinal wall into an outer primary tapetal cell, and a larger primary sporogenous cell (*fig. 6*). The primary tapetal cell may remain undivided, but usually it divides into two by an anticlinal wall. The plane of division is either parallel to the axis of the flower, as in *fig. 7*, or at right angles to this axis, as in *fig. 9*. The tapetal cells at once begin to lose their characteristic staining, and before their final disappearance are distinguishable from the other cells of the hypodermal layer only by their position. If, however, the primary tapetal cell does not divide, it retains its staining reaction more or less persistently to the last. The axial row of which the archesporium is the terminus also divides into two rows (*fig. 7*).

The further course of development of the primary sporogenous cell may be along two entirely different lines, which lead however to the same result, viz., the formation of a row of four megaspore mother cells, of which only the lowest one is fertile. These two series may be compared with those figured in Strasburger's *Angiospermen und Gymnospermen* for *Tritonia aurea* and *Anthericum ramosum* respectively. In the one case the primary sporogenous cell gives rise at once by successive divisions to a row of four cells, of which the lowest is always much the largest (*figs. 8* and *9*). In the other case, most common in Eichhornia, the elongation of the ovule is accompanied by an elongation of the primary sporogenous cell without division of the latter (*figs. 11* and *12*). The nucleus also enlarges and invariably remains at the apex. Some idea of the relative length of time during which this state of things continues may be gained by comparing the integuments of *figs. 7* and *8* with *10* and *11*.

The subsequent divisions in the elongated sporogenous cell take place in quick succession. I have obtained a very large number of karyokinetic figures of these divisions, for since Eichhornia is peculiar in having all the flowers of a spike in pretty nearly the same stage of advancement, a single spike may yield upwards of two thousand ovules all of nearly the same age. The first spindle is in the apex of the cell and the division is very unequal (*fig. 12*). There is no uniformity in the order in which the succeeding divisions occur. Sometimes the upper cell divides first, sometimes the lower; more rarely, as in *fig. 13*, they divide simultaneously. The spindle in the upper cell is almost always obliquely placed (it may even be transverse), and it is doubtful if cell division is ever completed or even a cell plate formed. The division in the lower cell is also unequal, so that the lowest cell of the four, the fertile mother cell, is from the very first quite as large as the three sterile ones together (*fig. 13*). From a study of a large number of cases, similar to *figs. 14* and *15*, I have been led to believe that the four mother cells when formed in this way are seldom, if ever, separated by walls.

All shades of transition between the two lines of megaspore development described above may easily be found even in the the same flower. Thus *figs. 11, 12, 13, 16, 17* and *18* are all from the same ovary. *Fig. 17* shows a case in which the first division of the primary sporogenous cell has taken place when it is about half grown. In *fig. 16* it will be seen that after the first division only the lower cell has lengthened and divided, and, though a division of the upper cell has begun, this has been stopped by the encroachment of the two cells below.

The three sterile mother cells, and after them the tapetal cells and other cells in the apex of the nucellus, are rapidly absorbed by the growing megaspore, which soon comes to abut directly against the epidermis. In the absorption of these cells there is no appearance of crowding; their walls break down and their protoplasm becomes continuous with that of the megaspore (*fig. 24*). Before the complete absorption of the tapetal cells the nucleus of the megaspore, situated about the middle of the cell, divides into two (*fig. 24*). The lower half of the megaspore at this time ceases to grow, while the upper half widens out and assumes the shape shown in *figs. 25–27*.

The division into micropylar and antipodal groups of four nuclei follows in the usual way without any regular time order. *Fig. 25* shows an embryo sac with four nuclei, *fig. 26* with eight nuclei, *fig. 27* fusion of the polar nuclei. The position of the definitive nucleus is always near the place where the embryo sac contracts into the narrow basal portion. This nucleus is large, has a very large, clear nucleolus, and is connected with the wall of the sac by strands of protoplasm. The fusion of the polar nuclei certainly occurs before pollination, for I have found the fusion accomplished in a flower whose perianth was not yet unclosed. That this act is not dependent upon the entrance of the pollen tube is proved very conclusively in *Caltha palustris*, where I have observed sterile ovules through whose thickened walls no pollen tube can pierce, yet whose embryo sacs always reach the seven-nuclear stage. In Eichhornia, also, the embryo sac always reaches the mature condition, in which, as we have seen, most of the pollen tubes break down without penetrating to the micropyle.

The antipodals of Eichhornia are evanescent, staining feebly from the first, and rarely with definite walls. Their nuclei do not divide either directly or by mitosis.

The egg apparatus has the usual arrangement. The synergids are provided with striated "filiform" tips and a prominent vacuole. The egg is relatively small and appears to be slung to the bases of the synergids (*figs. 28, 29*).

I have found a pollen tube reaching to the embryo sac in but one case, and that is represented in *fig. 29*. The single nucleus in the tip of the tube is probably one of the male nuclei, or possibly it is the generative nucleus itself, with which it agrees in size and staining. Its deep blue color is in strong contrast to the red of the synergids and oosphere, and of the tube nuclei of the microspores.

Since no embryos are formed the contents of the embryo sac sooner or later disorganize, always in this order : antipodals, synergids, oosphere, definitive nucleus. The definitive nucleus persists long after the other constituents of the embryo sac have disappeared. In a few instances a small number of free endosperm nuclei were found, and in one case these had arranged themselves into an incomplete parietal layer, but no cell formation of the endosperm was observed. Whether fertilization had been effected in these cases I could not make out, but the egg which was still intact had made no progress toward the development of an embryo. The coincidence of the usual failure of the pollen tube to penetrate to the oosphere with the infrequency of a division of the definitive nucleus lends weight to the generally accepted view that the stimulus which induces this division is the act of fertilization.

INTEGUMENTS OF THE OVULE.

The beginnings of the integuments may be seen in *figs. 6–8*. About the same time there begins a bending of the ovule which checks the growth of the outer integument where it comes in contact with the funiculus. By the time such a condition is reached as that shown in *fig. 12* the ovule is completely anatropous. The integuments are each two cell layers in thickness, with the cells above the micropyle much the largest. The absent portion of the outer integument next to the funiculus is represented by a thin layer of empty cells.

CYTOLOGY.

Only a few additional remarks need be made. I have not found Eichhornia a favorable subject for the study of cytological phenomena. Oil cells and glandular cavities are abundant, and a mucilaginous secretion pervades the cells and interferes with the transparency of the stains. Delafield's haematoxylin and erythrosin, and, in ovaries isolated from the perianth, anilin-safranin and gentian-violet gave the best results. Numerous other combinations were tried, but all were more or less unsatisfactory.

A typical spindle of the first karyokinesis of the elongated megaspore mother cell is represented in *fig. 20*. The large fibers attached to the chromosomes are plainly seen to be composed of many delicate threads. On the other hand the fibrillar structure of the central spindle is less clearly perceptible.

Cytoplasmic radiations about the poles occur in all good preparations and frequently the individual rays appear to terminate externally in large granules which stain like nucleoli. The chromosomes, 14 to 16 in number, were never seen to assume a V-shaped outline at any stage of the nuclear division. This statement holds good also for Pontederia, where by the use of iron-alum-haematoxylin a sharper definition of the chromosomes was secured.

All the preceding description of the spindle will apply equally to the divisions of the pollen mother cell.

The nucleus of the elongated sporogenous cell passes through a synapsis phase. If such a phase precedes the first division when that occurs early (as in *fig. 12*) I found no evidence of it. Perhaps no special significance can be assigned to the case shown in *fig. 18* (see also *figs. 22* and *23*), in which the two sporogenous cells whose nuclei are in synapsis have arisen apparently from the early division of the primary sporogenous cell. But if, as has been suggested by some cytologists, synapsis occurs only in those cells in which a reduction of the number of chromosomes is going on, it would follow that when the primary sporogenous cell divides early without elongating, the chromosome reduction takes place in each of the resulting nuclei; whereas if the primary sporogenous cell elongates before dividing, the reduction is completed in the first nucleus.

PONTEDERIA CORDATA.

Longitudinal sections of very young spikes furnished a complete series for the study of the organogeny of the flower. The order of succession of the floral organs is acropetal (*fig. 42*) and need not be dwelt upon. Both in stamens and carpels traces of zygomorphy are very early recognizable.

The first indication of the ovule is a slight swelling on the inner wall of the lowermost carpel which is always the smallest (*figs. 43, 43a*). Normally but one ovule makes its appearance. I had expected to find the beginnings of ovules in each of the three loculi, but the facts are otherwise; out of the hundreds of ovaries sectioned I found but seven cases of a second ovule beginning, and no case of a second ovule reaching maturity.

The various stages from the differentiation of an archesporial cell to the completion of the embryo sac can be followed easily in the plate (*figs. 44–53*). A few comments only will be necessary here. The dividing wall of the primary tapetal cell runs always, so far as I observed, in the same plane with reference to the axis of the flower. There is reason to believe that quite often but three megaspore mother cells are formed. The lengthening of the ovule is effected in part by an elongation of the epidermal and tapetal cells and the other cells of the nucellar apex (*figs. 45–47, 48–52*). Later, however, those cells of the nucellus which have escaped destruction by the growth of the megaspore divide transversely (*cf. figs. 48 and 53*). The bending of the ovule is at first in a plane passing through the axis of the flower. Afterwards the funiculus twists through an arc of ninety degrees so that the ovule comes to lie as shown in *fig. 45.*

The embryo sac is very poor in protoplasm. A large central vacuole is formed and the cytoplasm is pushed to the wall as a very thin layer (*figs. 50–52*). The egg apparatus is remarkably small and is crowded against the micropylar end. The definitive nucleus lies low down in the sac, and is suspended by the strings of protoplasm trailed together by the polar nuclei (*cf.*

figs. 52 and *53*). The antipodals here also are ephemeral, becoming very indistinct at the time of fertilization and soon after vanishing altogether.

The development of the microsporangia and microspores presents no unusual phenomena. As in Eichhornia the layer of cells outside the tapetum disintegrates before the latter and the tapetal cells are always uninucleate. *Figs. 57–65* represent stages in the division of the mother cells and growth of the microspores. Neither the generative nor the tube nucleus exhibits any of the abnormalities observed in Eichhornia.

The pollen tubes in their growth through the style are conducted along three canals which are each lined with a single layer of glandular cells (*fig. 55*). This layer is continued to the micropyle (*fig. 56*). The pollen tube entering the embryo sac was seen in several cases always passing between the synergids, one of which it destroys. Vestiges of the remaining synergid are still in view when the embryo has grown to such a size as in *figs. 67* and *68*. Apparently the pollen tube brings in two nuclei and its swollen end reaches almost, or quite, to the oosphere nucleus before these are set free (*fig. 54*).

A few stages of the young embryo are shown in *figs. 66–71*. The statement made in text-books that the roots of Pontederia have no dermatogen and hence no true epidermis applies only to the secondary roots. In the young embryo (see *figs. 70, 71*) a dermatogen is regularly cut off, and this in older embryos is continuous with the calyptrogen.

No attempt was made to study the cytology of Pontederia further than to determine the number of chromosomes, which is eight in the pollen mother cell, and fifteen or sixteen in the nuclei of the sporophyte tissue.

HETERANTHERA GRAMINIS.

A few ripe flowers of this species were sectioned and examined. In general appearance the ovule, with its integuments and embryo sac, bears a striking resemblance to those of Pontederia and Eichhornia. The synergids are longer and more prominent, however, and the embryo sac while smaller is more densely filled with protoplasm (*fig. 72*).

CONCLUSIONS.

I had hoped by a comparative study of closely related monocotyledons, and also of related dicotyledons, to be able in some degree at least to show how far the characters of the gametophyte generation could serve the purpose of indicating relationships among the larger groups of angiosperms. In this hope I have been disappointed. Those characters of the gametophyte generation in which, for example, Pontederia and Eichhornia agree, are characters which are common to hundreds of species of widely separated orders. The origin of the sporogenous tissue from the hypodermal cell terminating an axial row, the well-nigh universal occurrence of four megaspore mother cells of which but one matures, the usual cutting-off of a tapetal region which is finally absorbed by the growing megaspore, the division of the megaspore nucleus into eight free nuclei which are arranged in two groups of four each, the fusion of the polar nuclei to form a definitive nucleus which is the mother nucleus of the endosperm—these are the gametophytic characters of angiosperms in general. As soon as the comparison is pushed further we see that the differences between the two species in respect of the gametophyte are quite as great as often in other cases between unrelated plants, and the most striking resemblances, such as the shape of the ovule, embryo sac, and integuments are really sporophyte characters. If we were to draw up a tabular statement of the points in question in which Eichhornia and Pontederia agree, it would consist of two items : the ephemeral nature of the antipodals, which, however, is a characteristic of most monocotyledons; and the structure of the endosperm. Probably the female gametophyte of angiosperms has been so long parasitic upon the sporophyte that its only constant features are those of overwhelming phylogenetic importance, and its minor characters are readily variable in adaptation to the specific or generic differences of the sporophyte, or perhaps even to changes of environment. It seems, therefore, that the gametophyte characters cannot be of much value in assisting us to trace phylogenetic relationships among the angiosperms.

The irregularities which have been pointed out in Eichhornia may be correlated with its enormous power of vegetative reproduction. It has been propagated for years, without apparent loss of vitality, in the greenhouses and parks of Chicago, solely by this method; and no doubt this is its chief means of increase in the rivers of Florida and South America, where it has become a serious hindrance to navigation. The variations in the megaspore series are interesting, since they suggest how the megaspore of Lilium may have arisen from a type which had normally a tapetum and four megaspore mother cells. Let the change in Eichhornia go but a step further, let the nuclei which fail to form cells about themselves cease altogether to appear, and we should have a primary sporogenous cell passing without division into an embryo sac. Loss of the tapetum, as apparently occurs in *Hemerocallis fulva* by the same process (see the figures in *Angiospermen und Gymnospermen*), would result in the well-known habit of Lilium, where the archesporial cell develops directly into the embryo sac.

THE UNIVERSITY OF CHICAGO.

EXPLANATION OF PLATES XIX AND XX.

The plates have been reduced to ten twenty-sevenths of their original size. The magnifications given are those of the original drawings.

PLATE XIX.
Eichhornia crassipes.

FIG. 1. Longitudinal section of young ovary showing placenta. × 80.

FIG. 2. Cross section of an ovary of the same age as *fig. 1*. × 125.

FIG. 3. One of the placentæ of *fig. 2*. × 1300.

FIG. 4. Cross section of an older ovary. The cross indicates the position of the ovule which is shown in *fig. 5*. × 125.

FIG. 5. Longitudinal section of young ovule with archesporial cell. × 1300.

FIG. 6. An older ovule showing the primary tapetal cell (*t*) and primary sporogenous cell. × 1300.

FIG. 7. Ovule with primary sporogenous cell and two tapetal cells. × 1300.

FIG. 8. Ovule with two tapetal cells and two cells derived from division of the primary sporogenous cell. × 1300.

FIG. 9. Apex of nucellus with four mother cells. × 1300.

FIG. 10. Ovule showing primary sporogenous cell elongating. × 1300.

FIG. 11. Ovule with elongated primary sporogenous cell still undivided. × 825.

FIG 12. First division of the primary sporogenous cell. × 825.

FIG. 13. Second division in the megaspore series. × 1300.

FIGS. 14 and 15. Apex of nucellus with four megaspore mother cells. × 825.

FIGS. 16–19. Irregular development of the megaspore mother cells. × 825.

FIG. 20. Mitotic figure of first division of elongated primary sporogenous cell; cytoplasmic radiations about one pole. × 2000.

FIG. 21. Synapsis phase of the nucleus of the elongated primary sporogenous cell. × 2000.

FIGS. 22 and 23. The upper and the lower nucleus, respectively, of *fig. 18*, both in synapsis. × 2000.

FIG. 24. Apex of the nucellus with embryo sac after completion of first nuclear division. × 1300.

FIG. 25. The same after completion of second nuclear division. × 825.

FIG. 26. The same after completion of third nuclear division. × 625.

FIG. 27. Lower end of an embryo-sac showing the three antipodals, and fusion of the polar nuclei. × 1300.

FIG. 28. Embryo sac ready for fertilization. × 825.

FIG. 29. Apex of the embryo sac with pollen tube, striated synergids, and oosphere. × 1300.

FIG. 30. Part of cross section of anther; *t*, the tapetum. Outside the apetum a layer of disorganized cells may be seen. × 825.

FIG. 31. A single rounded pollen mother cell with its nucleus in the prophase stage. × 1300.

FIGS. 32–36*a*. Stages in the divisions of the pollen mother cell. *Fig. 32* shows the chromosomes in the equatorial plate of the first mitosis; *fig. 35* in the equatorial plate of the second mitosis. *Figs. 32 a* and *35* × 1550; the others × 1300.

PLATE XX.

FIG. 38. A microspore showing first organization of generative cell (*g*). In this and the following figures the tube nucleus is denoted by *t*. × 1300.

FIG. 39. Longitudinal section of an older microspore with generative cell and tube nucleus. × 1300.

FIG. 39 a. Cross section of microspore of same age as *fig. 39*. × 1300.

FIG. 40. Ripe microspore. × 1300.

FIG. 41. Longitudinal section of ripe microspore, with generative cell and two tube nuclei. × 1300.

FIG. 41 a. Cross section of a similar microspore. × 1300.

Pontederia cordata.

FIG. 42. Longitudinal section of young flower; *p*, perianth, *s*, stamen, *c*, carpel. × 125.

FIG. 43. Ovule before the differentiation of the archesporial cell. × 1300.

FIG. 43 a. Longitudinal section of ovary to show the relation of the ovule to the carpels.

FIG. 44. Young ovule with archesporial cell. × 1300.

FIG. 44 a. Longitudinal section of ovary to explain *fig. 44*.

FIG. 45. Cross section of ovary, semi-diagrammatic; *f*, vascular bundles, *g*, glandular cavities.

FIG. 46. Young ovule with tapetal cell (*t*) and primary sporogenous cell. × 1300.

FIG. 46. Young ovule. The primary tapetal cell has divided into two. × 1300.

FIG. 48. Apex of nucellus with four megaspore mother cells. × 825.

FIGS. 49 and 50. Encroachment of megaspore upon the sterile mother cells. At this time both integuments have grown beyond the apex of the nucellus. × 825.

FIG. 51. Embryo sac with two nuclei. × 825.

FIG. 52. Embryo sac with eight nuclei. × 825.

FIG. 53. Embryo sac ready for fertilization. × 825.

FIG. 54. Apex of embryo sac with pollen tube. × 1300.

FIG. 55. Longitudinal section of part of style, showing pollen tube traversing a cavity lined with glandular cells. × 825.

FIG. 56. Longitudinal section of ovary showing ovule, conducting tissue, and pollen tube (*p. t.*). × 125.

FIGS. 57–62. Stages in division of microspore mother cell. × 1300.

FIG. 59. Chromosomes in equatorial plate of first mitosis of microspore mother cell. × 1300.

FIGS. 64 and 65. Mature microspores. × 1300.

FIGS. 66–71. Stages in the early growth of the embryo; *d*, dermatogen. × 1300.

Heteranthera graminis.

FIG. 72. Embryo sac ready for fertilization. × 1300.

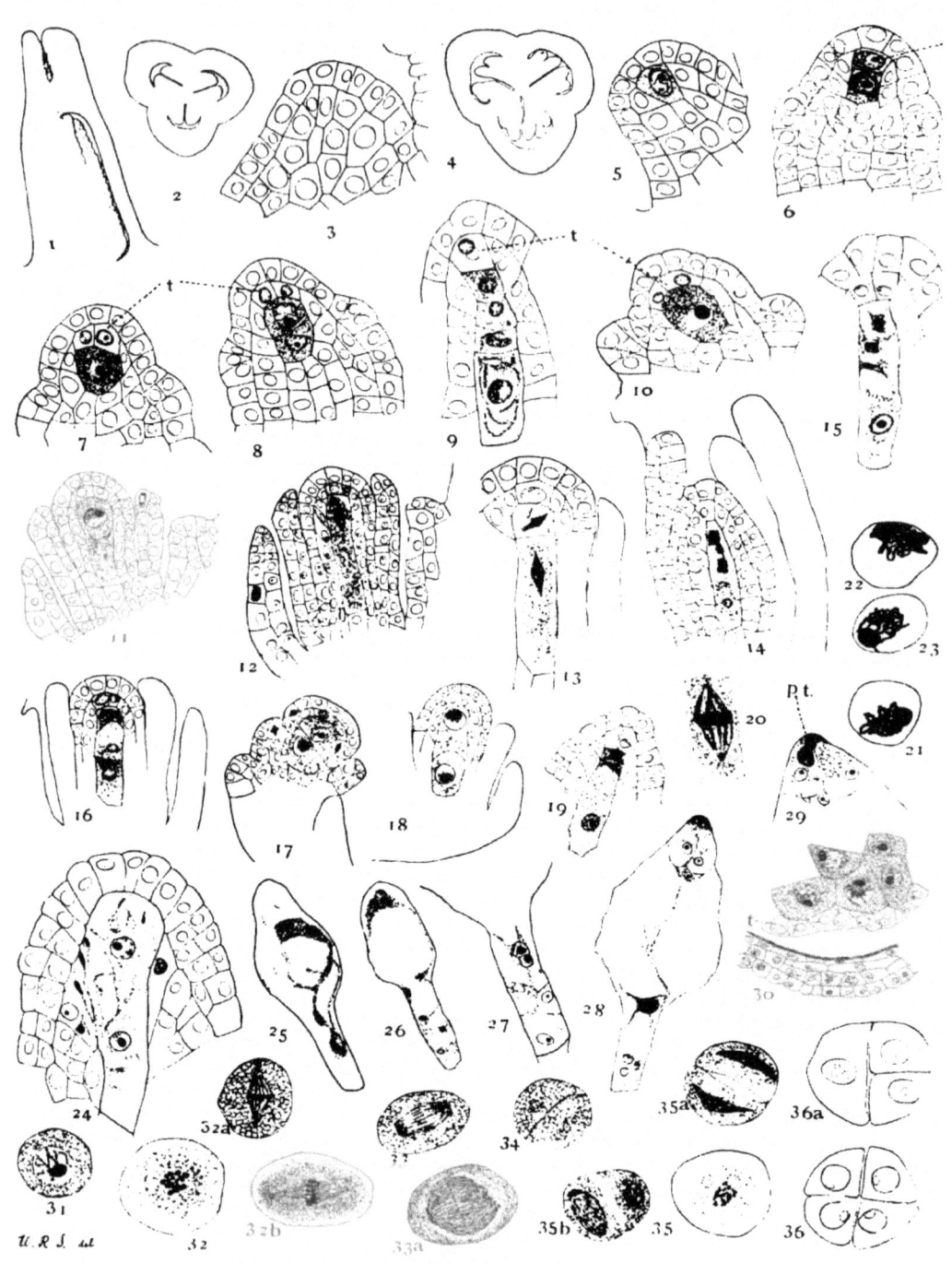

SMITH on PONTEDERIACEÆ.

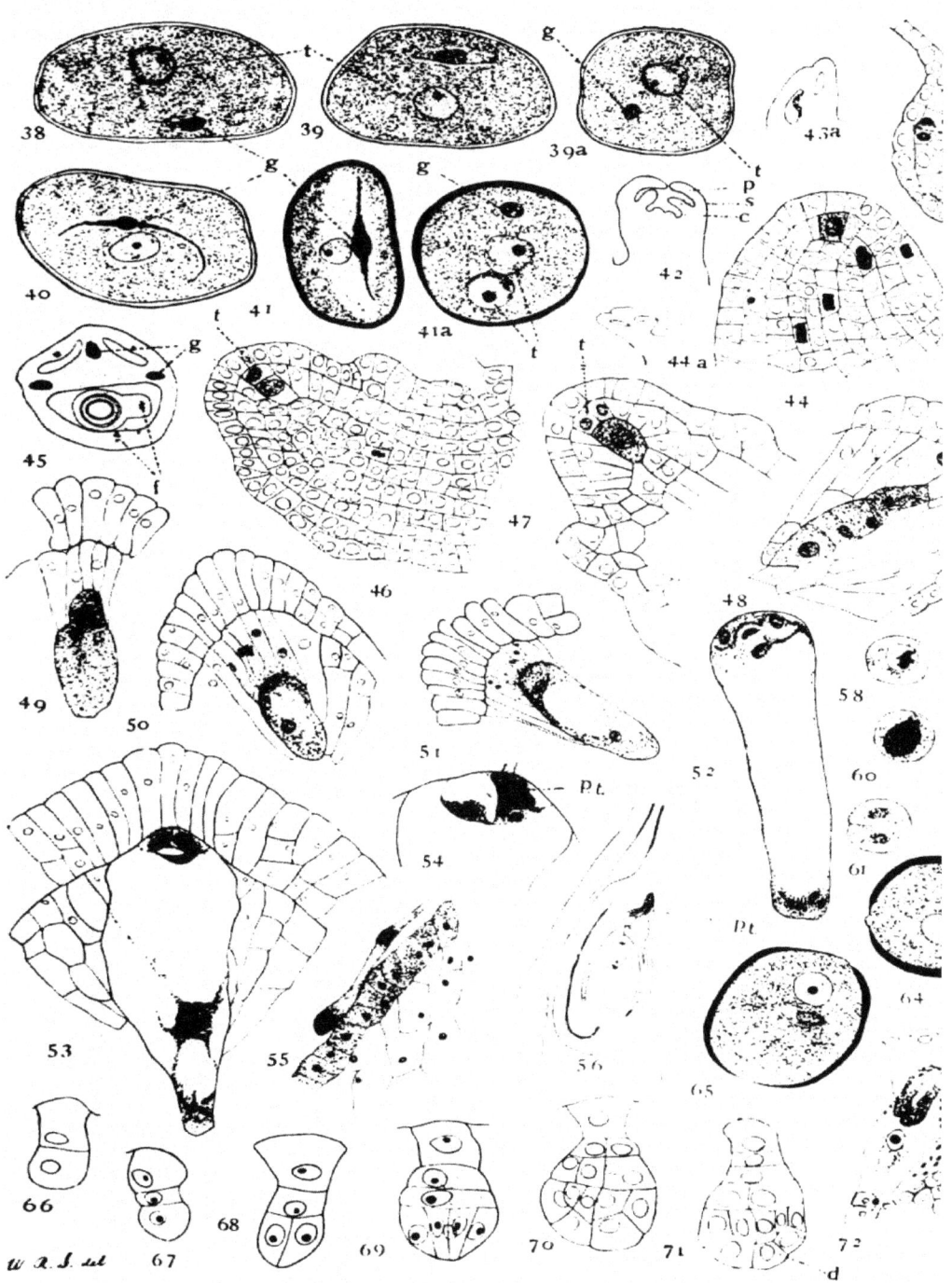

SMITH on PONTEDERIACEÆ.

LIBRARY USE

Check Out More Titles From HardPress Classics Series In this collection we are offering thousands of classic and hard to find books. This series spans a vast array of subjects – so you are bound to find something of interest to enjoy reading and learning about.

Subjects:
Architecture
Art
Biography & Autobiography
Body, Mind &Spirit
Children & Young Adult
Dramas
Education
Fiction
History
Language Arts & Disciplines
Law
Literary Collections
Music
Poetry
Psychology
Science
…and many more.

Visit us at www.hardpress.net

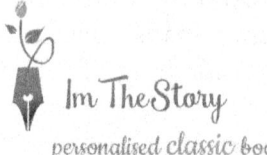

Im The Story
personalised classic books

"Beautiful gift.. lovely finish. My Niece loves it, so precious!"

Helen R Brumfieldon

★★★★★

UNIQUE GIFT
FOR KIDS, PARTNERS AND FRIENDS

Timeless books such as:

 Kids

Alice in Wonderland · The Jungle Book · The Wonderful Wizard of Oz
Peter and Wendy · Robin Hood · The Prince and The Pauper
The Railway Children · Treasure Island · A Christmas Carol

 Adults

Romeo and Juliet · Dracula

Highly Customizable · **Change** Books Title · **Replace** Characters Names with yours · **Upload** Photo for inside page · **Add** Inscriptions

Visit
ImTheStory.com
and order yours today!

CPSIA information can be obtained
at www.ICGtesting.com
Printed in the USA
BVHW040357280819
556943BV00034B/4067/P